DISCOVER
Science During the Renaissance

by Vickey Herold

Table of Contents

Introduction	2
Chapter 1 How Did Science Change During the Renaissance?	4
Chapter 2 What Did People Learn About Science?	8
Chapter 3 What Were the Inventions?	14
Conclusion	18
Concept Map	20
Glossary	22
Index	24

Introduction

The Renaissance was a time in history. The Renaissance was a time for **science**. The Renaissance was a time for change.

▲ Science changed during the Renaissance.

Words to Know

 compasses

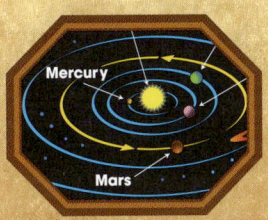 orbits

 scholars

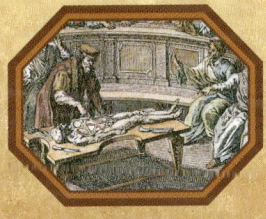 science

 telescopes

 the Renaissance

See the Glossary on page 22.

Chapter 1

How Did Science Change During the Renaissance?

Scholars had new ways to study.

▲ Scholars used new ways to study.

Scholars had new ways to learn.

▲ Scholars used new ways to learn.

Scholars had to use math.

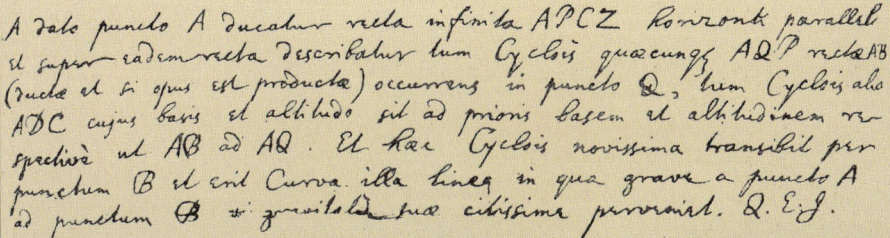
▲ Scholars used math.

Scholars had to use new tools.

▲ Scholars used new tools.

Chapter 1

Scholars had to find facts. Scholars had to use facts.

▲ Scholars used facts.

How Did Science Change During the Renaissance?

Scholars had to study facts. Scholars had to prove ideas.

It's a Fact
The scientific method began in the Renaissance. The scientific method began to prove ideas.

▲ Scholars used facts to prove ideas.

Chapter 2

What Did People Learn About Science?

People learned new things. People learned about the universe.

▲ People studied the universe.

People learned about Earth.

▲ People studied Earth.

People learned Earth moves around the sun.

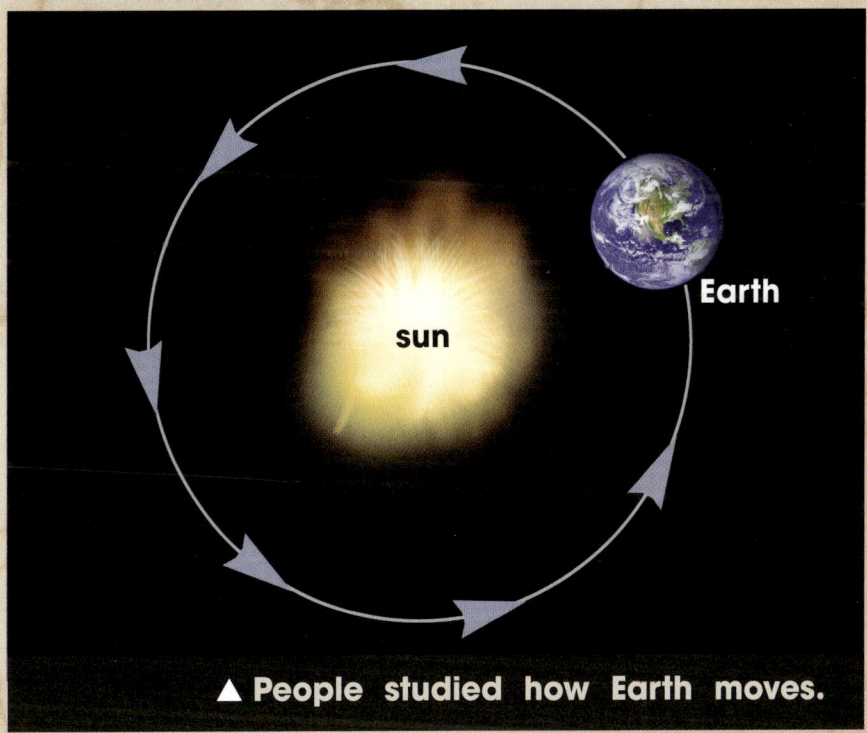

▲ People studied how Earth moves.

Chapter 2

People learned about the sun.

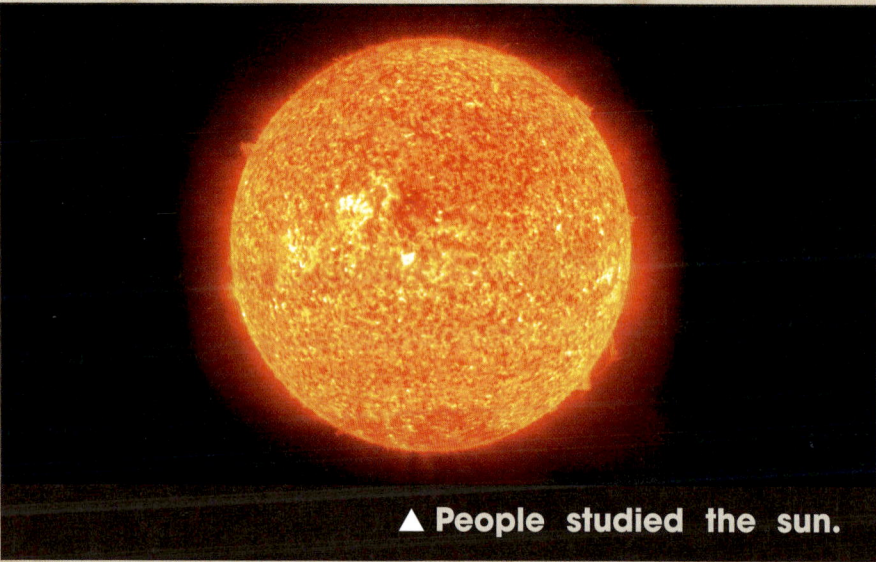

▲ People studied the sun.

People learned about planets.

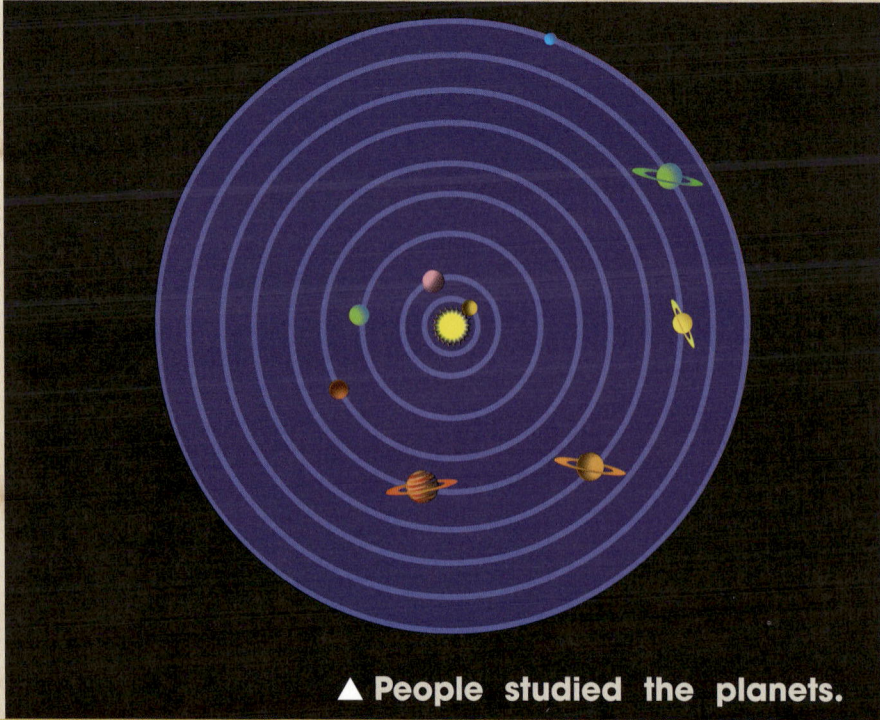

▲ People studied the planets.

What Did People Learn About Science?

People learned about **orbits**.

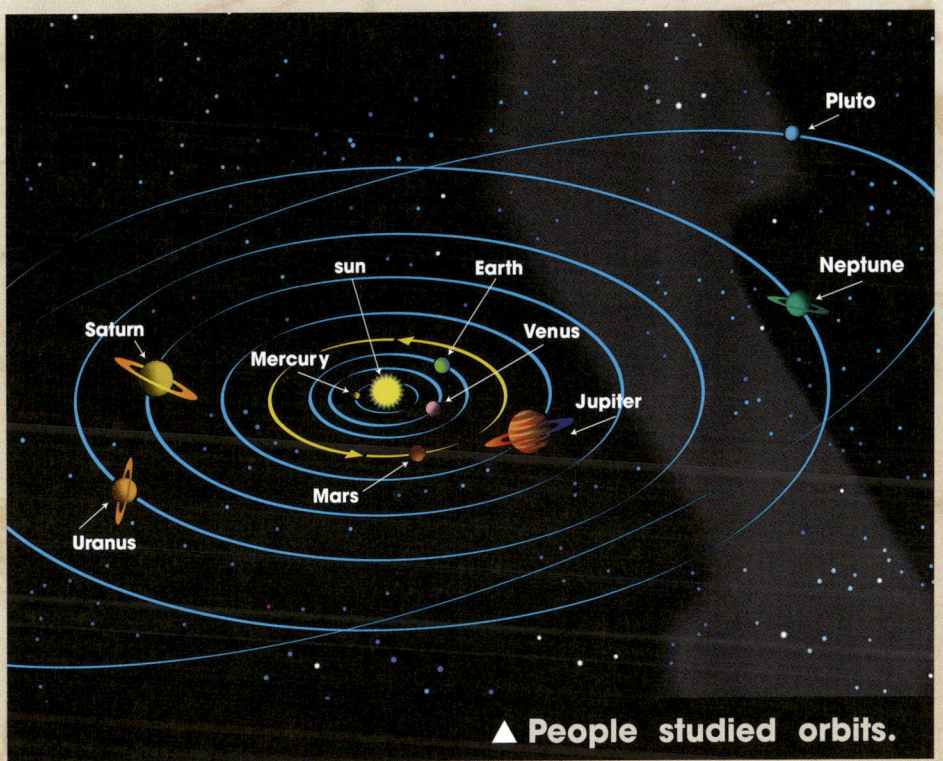

▲ People studied orbits.

It's a Fact

Galileo proved new ideas about the universe. Galileo proved Earth moves around the sun.

Chapter 2

People learned about the human body.
People learned how the body works.

▲ People studied the human body.

What Did People Learn About Science?

People learned about the skeleton.

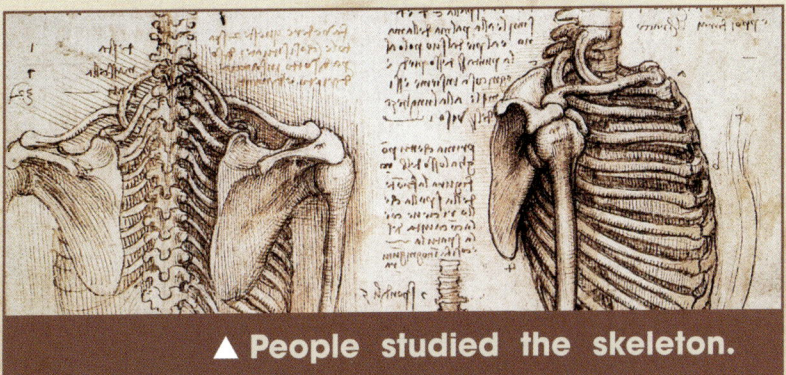

▲ People studied the skeleton.

People learned about the heart.

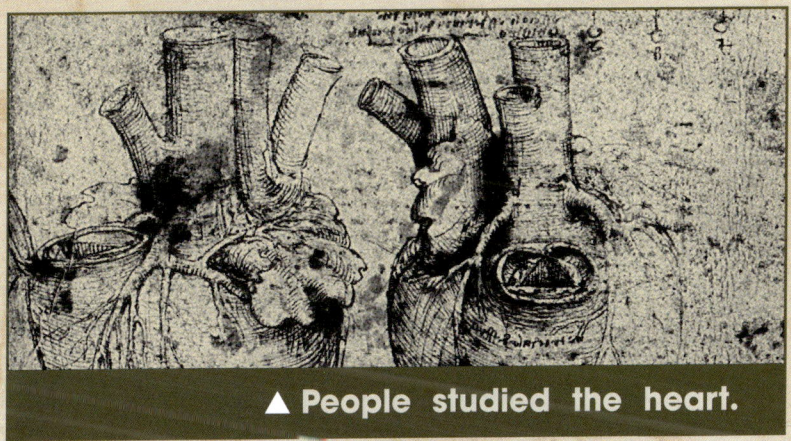

▲ People studied the heart.

People learned about the brain.

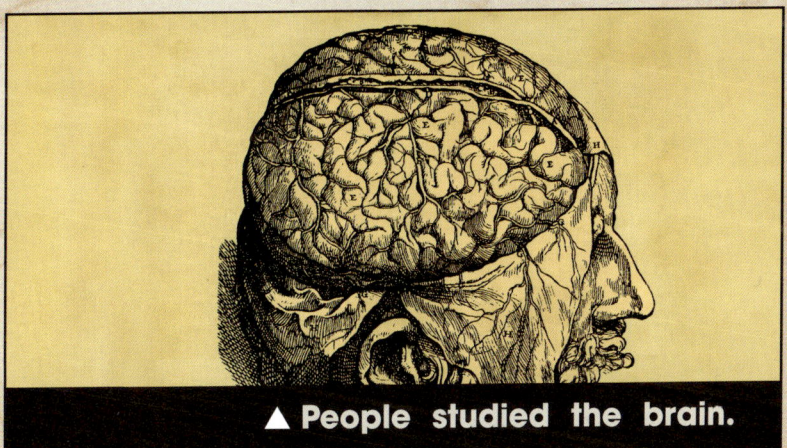

▲ People studied the brain.

Chapter 3

What Were the Inventions?

People made the printing press.

▲ The printing press was new.

People made books.

▲ The printing press helped people make books.

People made new **telescopes**.

▲ The telescope was new.

People made telescopes to study.

▲ Telescopes helped people study the universe.

Chapter 3

People made better **compasses**.

▲ Some compasses were new.

People made compasses to help explorers.

Did You Know?
Explorers sailed across oceans. Explorers sailed to the Americas.

▲ Some compasses helped explorers.

What Were the Inventions?

People made better maps.

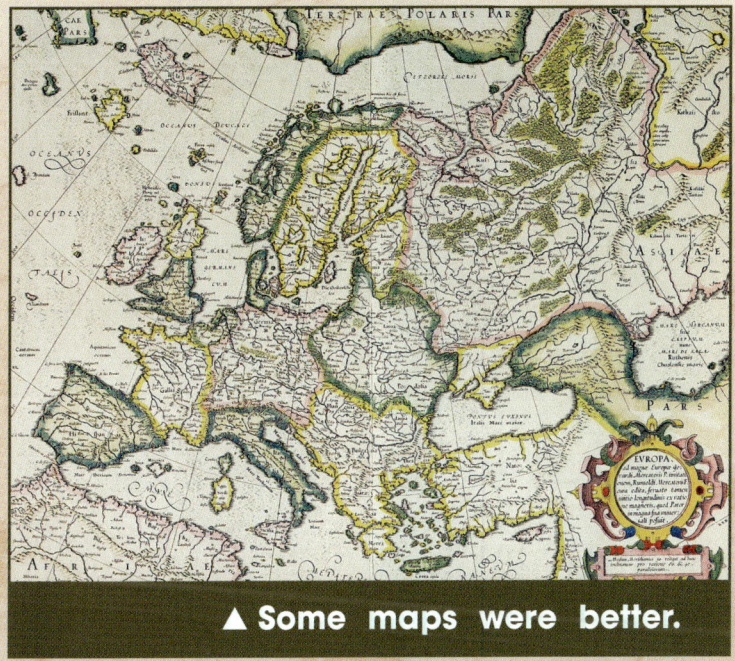

▲ Some maps were better.

People made maps of new lands.

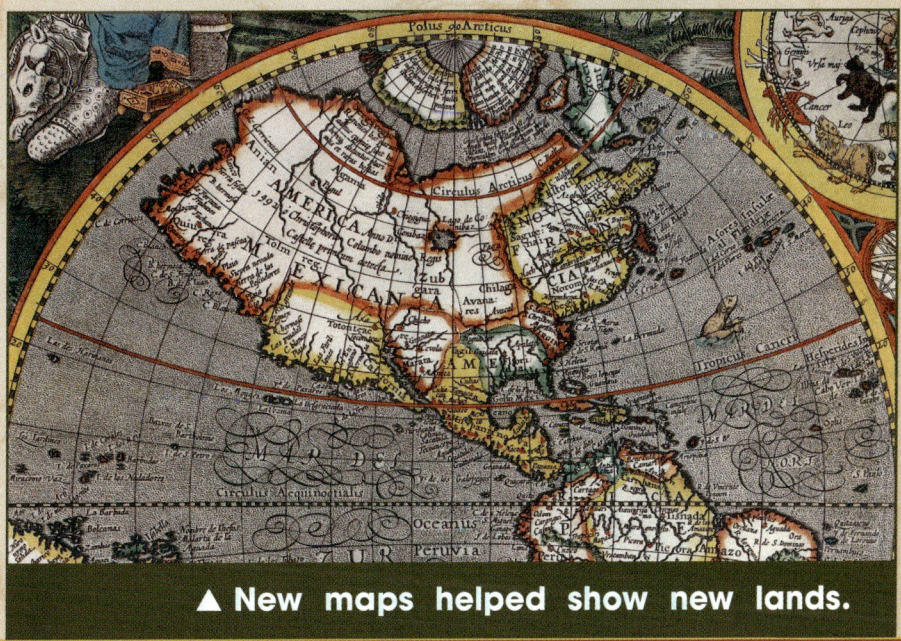

▲ New maps helped show new lands.

Conclusion

The Renaissance was a time to learn. The Renaissance was a time for science. The Renaissance was a time for inventions.

▲ The Renaissance was a time for learning.

Concept Map

Science During the Renaissance

How Did Science Change During the Renaissance?

- new ways to study
- new ways to learn
- used math
- used new tools
- used facts
- had to prove ideas

What Did People Learn About Science?

- about the universe
- facts about Earth
- facts about the sun
- facts about planets
- facts about orbits
- facts about the human body
- how the body works

What Were the Inventions?

| printing press |
| better compasses |
| telescopes |
| better maps |

Glossary

compasses tools people use to find directions

*People made better **compasses**.*

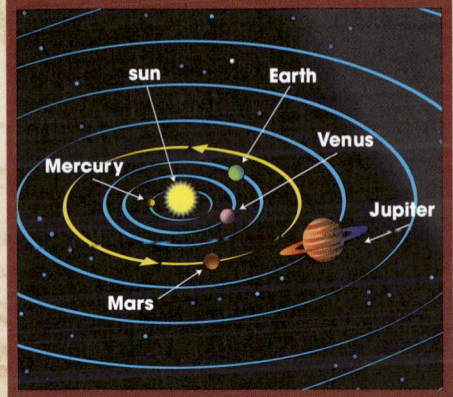

orbits paths followed around something

*People learned about **orbits**.*

scholars people with great knowledge

***Scholars** had new ways to study.*

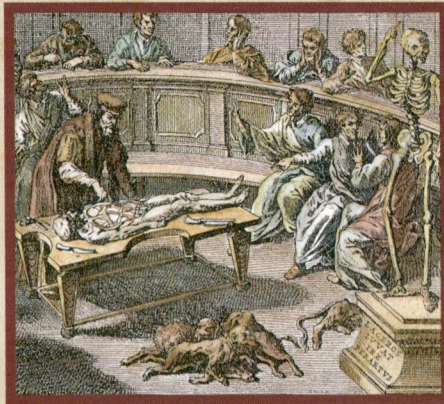

science an area of study

*The Renaissance was a time for **science**.*

telescopes tools people use to look at space

*People made new **telescopes**.*

the Renaissance a time in European history

***The Renaissance** was a time in history.*

Index

books, 14
brain, 13
compasses, 16
Earth, 9
explorers, 16
facts, 6–7
heart, 13
human body, 12
maps, 17
math, 5
new lands, 17
orbits, 11
planets, 10
printing press, 14
prove, 7
Renaissance, the, 2, 18
scholars, 4–7
science, 2, 18
skeleton, 13
sun, 9–10
telescopes, 15
tools, 5
universe, 8

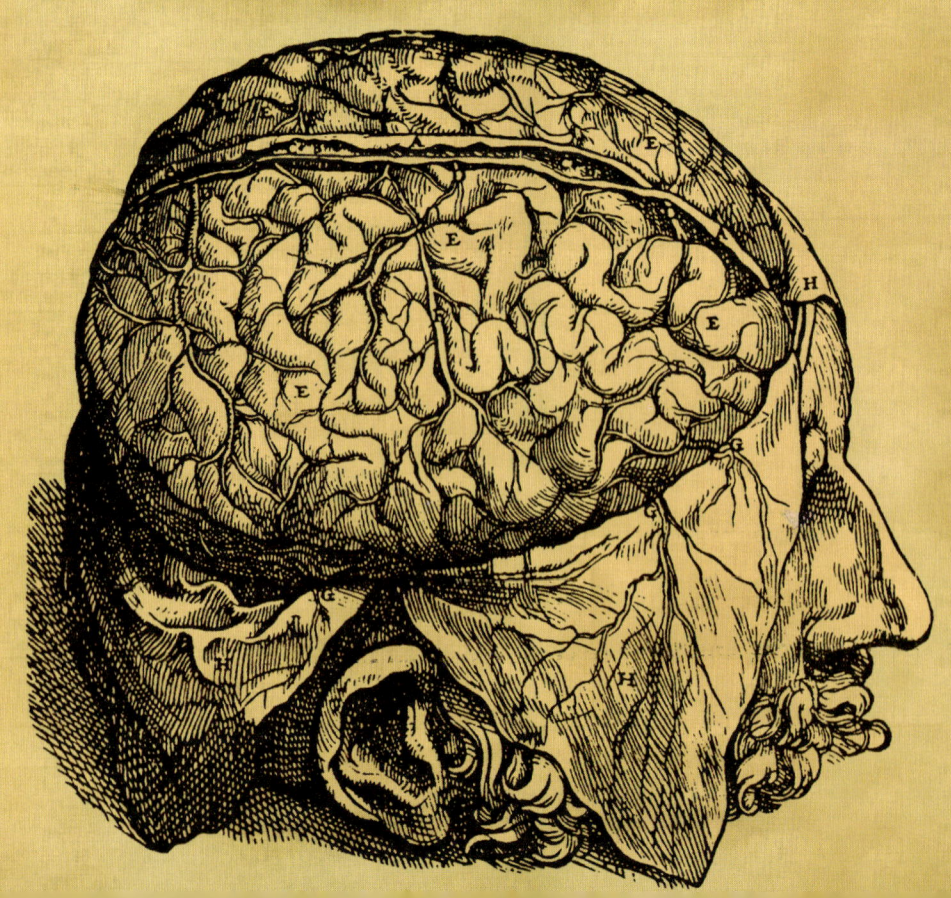